BOOK

5

All-American Series

'All Aboard' the Freedom Train

By Gene & Bobbie Carnell

© 2017 by innerQuest, an imprint of Chiron Publications. All rights reserved. No part of this publication may be reproduced, stored in a retrieval system, or transmitted, in any form by any means, electronic, mechanical, photocopying, recording, or otherwise, without the prior written permission of the publisher, Chiron Publications, 932 Hendersonville Road, Suite 104, Asheville, North Carolina 28803.

innerQuestBooks.com
ChironPublicatons.com

innerQuest is a book imprint of Chiron Publications
Edited by Jennifer Fitzgerald
Interior and cover design by Lisa Alford
Printed primarily in the United States of America.

If you are an organization wishing to buy bulk quantities of this book, please contact Chiron Publications at generalmanager@chironpublications.com

ISBN 978-1-63051-435-8 paperback

Library of Congress Cataloging-in-Publication Data Pending

Art courtesy of Freepik.com, Creative Commons, and the New York Public Library Digital Collection

Dedicated to all the hard-working parents
who provide for their families with
pride and dignity—and their parents
who inspired them beforehand.

All-American Series

Here's an old folk song as American as apple pie:

I've been working on the railroad,
All the live long day:
I've been working on the railroad,
just to pass the time of day.
Can't you hear the whistle blowing,
rise up so early in the morn?
Can't you hear the captain shouting,
Dinah, blow your horn?

We're travlin' on the Freedom Train,
And it will be a thrilling ride.
We'll meet America's heroes there,
And their stories will fill us with pride.
They'll tell of the price of liberty,
Of sacrifice and courage too!
We hope it'll make you feel as good as "US,"
To sing of the red-white-and blue!
-Uncle Sam's Version (GSC)

I bet you never took a train ride. If you haven't, you've missed a fun trip. It used to be the pace of living was slower and more relaxed. You can't see much of our country at 35,000 feet—or at 500+ miles per hour. What's the big hurry anyway?

The sights and sounds, the smells, the steam clouds and sleepy towns were unforgettable. Many happy memories were made riding the rails. Sadly, train travel is becoming a thing of the past.

Like many Americans, GEORGE PULLMAN found train travel difficult in the early years—there were no beds! So he remodeled railroad coaches with bunks that folded down at height for the passengers to climb into.

Then you could actually sleep on the train. The gentle swaying and "clickety-clack" would put you into a deep slumber in seconds.

Ask your parents to plan a vacation trip on one of those old "coal-burner" trains where you can ride for awhile—for a few minutes anyway. It would make a great family outing you'd never forget!

Before TV, politicians used the trains as rolling platforms to meet and greet the voters. They made "whistle-stops," brief visits to towns and cities across America. People would gather at the local train stations (depots) to hear their speeches, and then they'd move on down the track 15 or 20 miles to the next place.

It was a great tradition and served its purpose well.

Communication is very important to people's understanding of one another. Negotiations are better than confrontations. And the sharing and exchange of ideas, in civil tones, are what makes us stronger.

America was joined east and west by rail in 1869, at a place called Promontory Point in Utah, northwest of Salt Lake City.

Have you ever heard of "THE GOLDEN SPIKE?" Two companies, the Union Pacific (west) and the Central Pacific (east), raced across America in an "usual feat of engineering, vision, and courage."

The Central Pacific's engine was named Jupiter and burned wood. The Union Pacific's engine, #119, used coal for fuel. I hope you'll read about this adventure in a book entitled, "Nothing Like It In The World" by Stephen Ambrose, when you get a little older. It is exciting history!

FREEDOM TRAIN CROSSES AMERICA

Now I'd like to tell you about another special event called THE FREEDOM TRAIN. In the late 1940's, before any of you were born, and following World War II, a global conflict that threatened civilization's survival, a group of Americans were concerned.

They put together a little booklet about good citizenship and some historical exhibits on a train that went up and down and across parts of America. Why?

To remind us about the important aspects of our history and to inform young people about their rights and duties as well. Freedom is everybody's job!

When it came to your town, school children could walk through the cars where they were displayed and purchase little pamphlets for 25 cents to help offset the costs.

They even had ceramic cream pitchers with a decal of the train on it for sale, as a souvenir and keepsake.

We found one many years ago in an antique store we bought for $15. Many things increase in value with age. It was a moving experience in my life when my class toured it in 1948.

FREEDOM is like a train—a series of cars filled with people of high ideals pulling together for the common good.

It is powered by a strong engine over a precise route marked clearly with sturdy, unbending tracks. Our train's engine on The Liberty Express is fueled by the Rule of Law.

Its name is THE CONSTITUTION and it is a mighty unit. It too is old but still strong and solid having been on the job for many, many years.

Folk hero John Henry typifies the rugged determination of The American Spirit to cross all barriers and overcome all obstacles. He was a "steel-drivin" man!

The engine was followed by what was known as the "tender," where fuel was stored and could be shoveled into the boiler by a fireman. Tender is a good term and ours is the "caring car." Here the needs and concerns of society are brought to the attention of those running the train.

Each one is important and together they provide the power to make forward progress. Caring is the "fuel" that keeps us all "on track!"

You may not have known about this other kind of "fireman." You're probably familiar with the ones who lost their lives at the World Trade Center in New York. But every person has a role to fill and a job to do. Our fireman shovels coal; or feeds the boiler with wood to make steam.

Next are found the passenger cars on our "Express." They are filled with citizens who pay their fares and look to the engineer and crew to get them to their destination safely and on time. This includes people like your parents or neighbors, postman, minister, or rabbi. And lots of children too.

Most people are friendly and smiling; others don't look or act too happy. Still, they are our fellow travelers and regardless of what they do, we should enjoy the trip. We may even be able to cheer them up if we try.

These are followed by the dining car. This is something we are fortunate to do at least three times a day in America. In many parts of the world children go to bed hungry. Why is there enough food for all the passengers on our train?

Because many people had a part in providing and preparing good, healthy menus: farmers who grow the food; plants that process it; truckers who transport it; chefs who cook it; and servers in crisp white jackets who bring it to the table for us.

FARMERS

PASSENGERS
(consumers)

PROCESSING
PLANTS

WAITERS & SERVERS

TRUCKERS

CHEFS
(cooks)

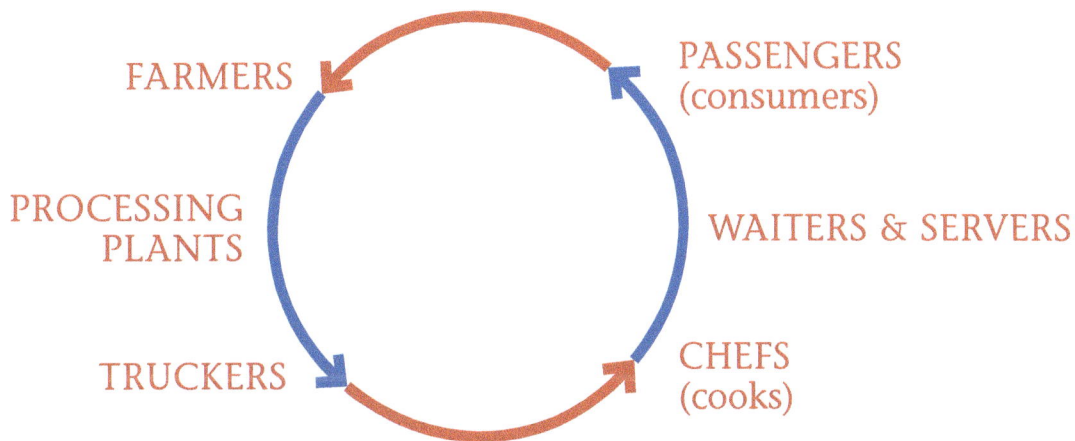

It's a big operation but a good example of co-operation!

Maybe that's where the saying,
"The wheels of progress keep turning"
comes from.

There are many good Americans working hard everyday to care for their families. Have you decided what you are going to do to make a living and provide for your family when you grow up?

At the end of trains in olden days was a cute little red car called a "caboose," where the crew could relax when it took a break.

This is an English word for "ship's galley." And a ship galley is a ship's kitchen. Wow!

The signalman stayed in the caboose. His job always put him at the back of the train. With a flag in the daytime and a lantern at night, he would tell the engineer way up at the front when to go forward or back up. He "lived" in the caboose; cooked his meals and slept there. His self-reliance urged on and directed those ahead. Sounds like democracy to me!

Remember, our "chugging-along, persistent type of government" resembles a train: hooked together; going in the same direction; helping others keep in line; traveling along as one unit.

There is a lesson in per-sev-er-ance too. This is a big word which means "KEEPING-ON-KEEPING-ON!" Staying on the job till the journey's done.

Let's do it until we get it right. And if it works—don't fix it. But, boys and girls, FREEDOM is a work-in-progress—employing heroes and citizens alike! Let's all keep The Liberty Express on the track and rolling ahead on schedule. And you know what?

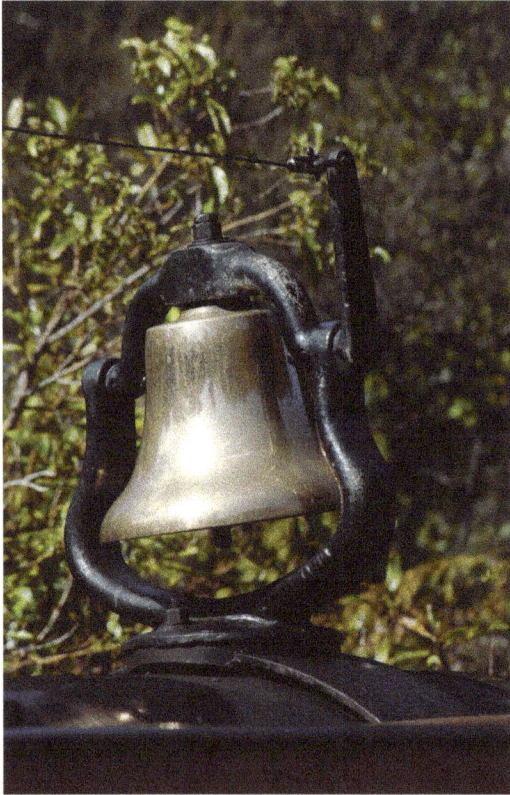

Any one of you reading this book could be the next engineer. That's True!

On the top of the engine was a huge bell. Model railroaders tell us the whistle was to let others know the train was coming. The bell signaled when it was going to leave: "Clear-the-tracks!" Clang! Clang! Get ready! The conductor calls, "All Aboard!" and we're off.

Do you like bells? I do. They make a wonderful sound. They are pleasant to hear and are used to announce important events and information—and even to celebrate with. Remember, we've already talked about "The Bell" in our first book, right?

Here's some more important information about that famous bell. Once upon a time, in America's past—on a rainy day in Pennsylvania—this bell signaled "All Aboard" for a new adventure. As shadows of civil unrest thickened, the SECOND CONTINENTAL CONGRESS sensed the seriousness of the situation.

They designated May 17, 1776, as a day of national fasting and prayer. "Fasting" is a spiritual discipline— doing without usual things so one could concentrate on higher things for a day.

And they asked John Witherspoon, a gifted preacher, to deliver the message, which he did, about "The Dominion of Providence Over the Affairs of Men."

It was a moving experience in which he spoke about God's eternal purposes and man's precious gift of liberty. Still the important question of whether to declare independence (self rule), from Britain or not stood in doubt. A final vote would be taken in early July.

DETROIT PHOTOGRAPHIC CO., PUBLISHERS.

6078. OLD LIBERTY BELL.

While patriots debated inside, outside in the streets people gathered in little groups to learn of the outcome. All were talking and very concerned. "Where were the colonies headed on a trackless path? And would the journey be dangerous?"

In the steeple of the Old State House in Philadelphia was the huge bell on which was etched this inscription from the Bible:

> PROCLAIM LIBERTY THROUGHOUT THE LAND
> TO ALL ITS INHABITANTS.
> (Leviticus 25:10)

In the morning, the bell-ringer went to his post in the tower having stationed his apprentice (helper) below to await the decision so that his bell might be the first to peal forth the glad tidings—or bad news—depending upon the vote of those early citizens who treasured freedom more than a false security.

The lad paced back and forth shaking his head and mumbling to himself, "They will never do it; they will never do it!"

Suddenly the old man above heard the lad below clapping out: "Ring! Ring!"

LIBERTY EXPRESS was getting underway! Grabbing the heavy iron tongue, he swung it with all his might over and over announcing the good news of "liberty to all the land."

Some say his enthusiasm cracked the giant sentinel we know as The Liberty Bell although that actually happened earlier—in fact, the very first time it rang. It was scarred but still strong. But Let Freedom Ring!

Let me tell you now about a lovely lady I knew one time from the state of Virginia, sometimes called "The Mother of Presidents." Eight U.S. presidents were born there including four of the first five: Washington, Jefferson, Madison, and Monroe.

She was the pianist in my church and played faithfully for many years. She was also a good friend and an excellent poet. Here's one she wrote on "The Bell of Freedom".

LET FREEDOM RING,

Let countless thousands ring that bell,

Then hear the wondrous things they tell,

Their songs of freedom sing.

O dare not say we are not free,

Those priceless things are ours to hold;

What'er we choose, we're free to see—

Trees or flowers or sunset's gold,

Free to tell the truth or lie,

We're free to choose the right or wrong:

Free to worship God on high.

Dare not deny that precious right,

To hold on high th' eternal light—

Let Freedom Ring!

—Anita F. Hurst, July 4, 1968
Vienna, VA & Flagler Beach, FL

Words joined with music become songs, and the music of America represents our common bonds and commitment to positive ideals. Patriotic songs remind us all of our heritage and our dependence upon Divine Providence for the untold blessings we all enjoy. Sadly, you don't hear much about this special relationship today, but folks back then lived and died by these truths.

We're rapidly approaching our destination. Aunt Samantha and I sincerely hope you have enjoyed our "All-American Adventure" together. We know we have.

To review where we've been, we looked first at **The Symbols of Freedom**, those signposts and monuments along our journey. If "One picture is worth a thousand words" you'll never forget their historical importance.

Our second trip, **The Big Picture**, introduced you to all the exciting possibilities you have because you live in this great nation.

Always try to be your best and do your best as a responsible adult citizen. Not everyone in the world enjoys the same degree of freedom!

The Big Parade showed us how important it is that we work together, and just how much more enjoyable each experience can be when shared with others in our communities.

Remember, celebrating special events from America's past gives stability and meaning to the present—not to mention the fun! *VICTORY at the Vets* was our favorite, I think, because so many good things happened at Dr. Joan's clinic.

Of course, we love animals like you guys. We hope you saw that there is great power in team work. When we put someone else's problems ahead of our own, amazing things happen. It really does bring out the best in us.

And *"All-Aboard" The Freedom Train* brought back a lot of good warm memories for me. It was one of the best, most positive influences of my childhood.

Actually, we are what we've been! All the experiences we have, all of the things we learn, all of the right examples we see tend to mold us and shape us into what we ought to be as grown-ups and good citizens.

We hope you will keep this series intact and one day share it with your children. God Bless You and God Bless America!

Uncle Sam and Aunt Samantha

"We are sojourners together in this beautiful land.
Let's do our part to keep it strong and make it grand."
-Aunt Samantha

LESSONS FOR LIFE

1. The journey can be as much fun as the destination.
2. Life is a gift to be invested—never wasted.
3. Teamwork makes everyone better.
4. Each day is filled with exciting events.
5. Dream big! Aim high! Stand tall!

THE AMERICAN'S CREED

I believe in the United States of America, as a government of the people, by the people, for the people; whose just powers are derived from the consent of the governed; a democracy in a republic; a sovereign Nation of many sovereign States; a perfect union, one and inseparable; established upon these principles of freedom, equality, justice, and humanity for which American patriots sacrificed their lives and fortunes. I therefore believe it is my duty to my country to love it, to support its Constitution, to obey its laws, to respect its flag, and to defend it against all enemies.

— Statement written in 1917 by William Tyler Page as an entry into a patriotic contest and passed as resolution by the U.S. House of Representatives on April 3, 1918.

www.ingramcontent.com/pod-product-compliance
Lightning Source LLC
Chambersburg PA
CBHW051310020426
42331CB00018B/3489